Daily Activity Bank

SOCIAL STUDIES

SCOTT FORESMAN

SCOTT FORRESMAN

★ ALL TOGETHER ★

W9-AHB-826

Scott Foresman

Editorial Offices: Glenview, Illinois • Parsippany, New Jersey • New York, New York
Sales Offices: Parsippany, New Jersey • Duluth, Georgia • Glenview, Illinois • Coppell, Texas • Ontario, California

www.sfsocialstudies.com

Contents

ISBN 0-328-03919-5

2 3 4 5 6 7 8 9 10 V008 10 09 08 07 06 05 04 03 02

Fast Fact 1

The United States is made up of 50 states.

What are the names of two states that do not touch any other state?

Geography

History

Fast Fact 2

The first library for children opened in Salisbury, Connecticut, in 1803.

How do you check out a library book?

Fast Fact 3

Abraham Lincoln is pictured on the penny.

What are some coins that have pictures of buildings on them?

Economics

Government Citizenship

Fast Fact 4

A letter carrier delivers mail even when the weather is bad. A letter carrier will also pick up your mail and send it for you.

How would someone address a letter to be delivered to you?

Fast Fact 5

Many Chinese children celebrate the Chinese New Year by dressing in new clothes and joining in a huge parade led by a silk dragon.

How do you celebrate the New Year?

Culture

Geography

Fast Fact 6

The Pacific Ocean is the world's largest ocean.

What color is an ocean on a map?

Fast Fact 7

President Andrew Johnson never attended school. His wife encouraged him to read and helped him learn to write and do math.

Why may a person not be able to go to school?

History

Economics

Fast Fact 8

Some farmers sell fresh fruits and vegetables at roadside stands.

Where else can you buy fruits and vegetables?

Fast Fact 9

President Ulysses S. Grant was arrested for riding his horse too fast through Washington, D.C., and was fined $20.

What might happen today if you drove a car too fast?

Government
Citizenship

Culture

Fast Fact 10

The kiwi fruit was brought to New Zealand from China and named after the national bird of New Zealand, the kiwi bird. Kiwi birds cannot fly!

What is the national bird of the United States?

Fast Fact 11

Three states, Iowa, Ohio, and Utah, have names with only four letters.

Write the name of your state. How many letters are there?

Geography

Fast Fact 12

The Teddy Bear is said to be named after President Theodore Roosevelt. While on a hunting trip, President Roosevelt refused to shoot a bear cub.

What is a nickname for Theodore?

Fast Fact 13

People on the Pacific Island of Fiji used whales' teeth as money until the early 1900s.

What else might you use for money?

Economics

Government Citizenship

Fast Fact 14

The United States flag has 13 stripes and 50 stars.

How many stripes are red? How many stripes are white?

Fast Fact 15

Italian people used to celebrate by throwing confetti, or candies wrapped in colored paper. Today people still celebrate by throwing confetti only now it is just colored bits of paper.

When might people throw confetti?

Culture

Geography

Fast Fact 16

More people live in New York City than in any other city in the United States.

What ocean is near New York City?

Fast Fact 17

Christopher Columbus's first trip across the Atlantic Ocean, from Spain to San Salvador, took 70 days.

How was Christopher Columbus traveling?

History

Economics

Fast Fact 18

Dimes, quarters, half dollars, and dollar coins look like silver but are a mixture of copper, nickel, and other metals.

Which of these coins is the smallest in size?

Fast Fact 19

Abraham Lincoln was often called "Honest Abe."

Tell about a time when you were honest.

Government
Citizenship

Culture

Fast Fact 20

Bricks of clay and straw dried in the sun are called adobe. Some people in the Southwest live in adobe homes.

What else can be used to build homes?

Fast Fact 21

California has more people, more cars, more schools, and more businesses than any other state in the United States.

What is the name of a large city in California?

Geography

History

Fast Fact 22

The Pilgrims, founders of Plymouth, Massachusetts, landed in America on December 21, 1620.

What was the name of the ship on which the Pilgrims sailed from England?

Fast Fact 23

Bananas do not grow on trees; they are really giant herbs. The banana is also one of the few fruits that ripens best after it is picked.

You can buy a bunch of bananas. What else can you buy in bunches?

Economics

Government Citizenship

Fast Fact 24

The President not only lives in the White House, the President works there too! The President's office is called the Oval Office.

Draw a large oval, the shape of the President's office. Inside the oval draw things that you would find in an office.

Fast Fact 25

The Children's Museum in Boston, Massachusetts, has a full-size Japanese house and a Latino market.

What is a museum?

Culture

Geography

Fast Fact 26

Alaska is the largest state in the United States.

What is the smallest state?

Fast Fact 27

The first car was made in Germany more than 100 years ago. Its top speed was 10 miles per hour!

How are cars today different from cars made long ago?

History

Economics

Fast Fact 28

The motto of the United States, "In God We Trust," is placed on all paper money and coins.

Find the motto on a penny and a dime. Where does the motto appear on each coin?

Fast Fact 29

The President of the United States serves a four-year term. No President can be elected more than twice.

Who is the President of the United States today?

Government Citizenship

Culture

Fast Fact 30

Many Irish Americans celebrate Irish traditions on St. Patrick's Day. Traditional celebrations include parades and the wearing of green.

Ireland is sometimes called the Emerald Island. What color is an emerald?

Fast Fact 31

The Great Salt Lake is the largest saltwater lake in North America.

What is another body of water that is salty?

Geography

History

Fast Fact 32

Long ago people who could not read or write signed their name with an *X*.

What do you think it would be like to be an adult who could not read or write?

Fast Fact 33

The first computer filled a large room because its electronic parts were so big.

Tell about computers of today. How do they look? How are they used?

Economics

Fast Fact 34

President Franklin Roosevelt was the first President to appear on both radio and television.

Why is it important for the President to communicate with people in our country?

Fast Fact 35

Christmas, Hanukkah, Kwanzaa, and St. Lucia Day are all holidays in which candles are used as important symbols.

What can you tell about a holiday where there are candles?

Culture

Geography

Fast Fact 36

The small country of Singapore has the same name as its capital city, Singapore.

What is the name of the capital city of the United States?

Fast Fact 37

The United States of America declared its independence, or freedom, from Great Britain in 1776.

On what day each year do people celebrate Independence Day?

History

Economics

Fast Fact 38

In the 1600s Pilgrim children had to work hard. Their chores probably included fetching water from a stream, gathering firewood, herding animals, and finding berries and other wild plants for food.

What jobs do you do to help your family?

Fast Fact 39

Your fingerprints can be used to identify you because everyone's fingerprints are different. Everyone's footprints are also different!

How do you think the police might use fingerprints?

Government
Citizenship

Culture

Fast Fact 40

The first televised tour of the White House was led by First Lady Jacqueline Kennedy in 1962.

What are two news events that you have seen on television?

Fast Fact 41

The coldest recorded temperature is 129 degrees below zero. This temperature was recorded at Antarctica.

Is the South Pole or the North Pole located on Antarctica?

Geography

History

Fast Fact 42

President John Adams was the first President to live in the White House. When he moved in, the freshly painted walls were still wet!

Name the city where the White House is located.

Fast Fact 43

Chicago's central business district is called *the Loop* because of the raised train tracks that circle the area.

What kind of workers might you find in the business district of a large city?

Economics

Fast Fact 44

In 1872, Susan B. Anthony was arrested in Rochester, New York, for attempting to vote. She was fined $100, which she never paid.

What does it mean to vote?

Fast Fact 45

New York's Coney Island was home to the first roller coaster, *the Switchback Railway*, about 120 years ago.

Coney Island was the name of an amusement park. What might you see at an amusement park today?

Culture

Geography

Fast Fact 46

Vermont produces more maple syrup than any other state in the United States.

What kind of trees would you tap for maple syrup?

Fast Fact 47

In 1809 James Madison was the first President to wear long trousers daily. The three Presidents before Madison all wore short trousers that fastened below the knee!

How has clothing changed since James Madison was President?

History

Economics

Fast Fact 48

The United States Mint was founded in 1792 and makes all of the pennies, nickels, dimes, quarters, half dollars, and dollar coins that we use.

Whose face is pictured on a quarter?

Fast Fact 49

Every country has its own set of laws. In England, the law says that people must drive on the left side of the road. In the United States, people must drive on the right side of the road.

Why are laws important?

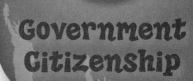

Government Citizenship

Culture

Fast Fact 50

A fiesta is often held to celebrate Mexican Independence Day. During a fiesta there may be colorful parades, music, dancing, spicy foods to eat, fireworks, a bullfight, or a rodeo.

What might you see at a rodeo?

Fast Fact 51

The first electric red and green traffic lights were invented and installed in Cleveland, Ohio, in 1914.

Find Ohio on a map. What lake is next to Ohio?

Geography

Fast Fact 52

An animal lending library opened in Sacramento, California, in 1951. After children were shown how to care for the animal, they could check it out for seven days!

Do you think an animal lending library is a good idea? Why or why not?

Fast Fact 53

A coin lasts for about 25 years. Coins that are worn-out are sent to the United States Mint where they are melted and made into new coins.

What are the names of four different coins?

Economics

Government Citizenship

Fast Fact 54

The American flag should never touch the ground or the floor.

What are other ways to show respect for the American flag?

Fast Fact 55

In 1853 a Native American chef at a hotel in Saratoga Springs, New York, made the first potato chips. They were called Saratoga chips!

What name do you think is better, Saratoga chips or potato chips? Why?

Culture

Geography

Fast Fact 56

Canada is the world's second largest country in size and covers more than half of North America.

Canada borders the United States on the north. What is the name of the country that borders the United States on the south?

Fast Fact 57

Pioneer children played with dolls made of cornhusks and built toy log cabins with corncobs.

What are some toys that you could make at home today?

History

Economics

Fast Fact 58

Every coin or bill that the government makes has the year it was made stamped or printed on it.

Look at a coin or a bill and find the date. What year was the coin or bill made?

Fast Fact 59

The Statue of Liberty is one of the largest sculptures in the world. It is so big that people can walk around inside it and climb up to its head!

What is the Statue of Liberty holding in her raised hand?

Culture

Fast Fact 60

The Aloha Festival is Hawaii's largest festival and lasts for two months. It is a celebration of music, dance, and history.

Aloha is a Hawaiian word. Look up *aloha* in a dictionary and tell what it means.

Fast Fact 61

In the state of Florida, there are more than 30,000 lakes. Some of these lakes have alligators!

What large bodies of water touch Florida's coasts?

Geography

History

Fast Fact 62

In 1900 horses pulled the wagons that delivered ice and bottles of milk. Horse-drawn wagons also carried water to put out fires.

What better ways of putting out fires do we have today?

Fast Fact 63

Peanuts grow underground and are called groundnuts or goobers.

What are some products made from peanuts?

Economics

Government Citizenship

Fast Fact 64

The Liberty Bell, a symbol of freedom, was rung every July 4th and on special occasions until a large crack formed that affected the sound of the bell.

Why was the Liberty Bell rung every year on July 4th?

Fast Fact 65

In many Asian countries it is a custom to remove your shoes at the door before entering a home.

Think of other everyday customs, such as sharing meals or reading bedtime stories. What are some of your favorite customs?

Culture

Geography

Fast Fact 66

Fewer people live in Australia than live in the state of Texas.

Look at a map. What are the names of three large cities in the state of Texas?

Fast Fact 67

New York City was the first capital of the United States.

Washington, D.C., is the capital of the United States today. What river runs through Washington, D.C.?

History

Economics

Fast Fact 68

A nickel was once called a half-dime and was exactly half the size of a dime!

How has the nickel changed?

Fast Fact 69

Every person is expected to obey the laws of the community, state, and country where he or she lives. People are also expected to respect the rights of others.

What does it mean to respect the rights of others?

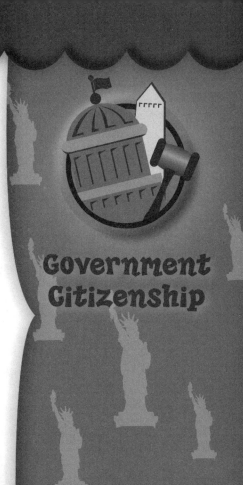

Government Citizenship

Culture

Fast Fact 70

Fast food is an American way of life. Every day, Americans munch through seven million pizzas!

What are other fast foods that Americans eat?

Fast Fact 71

All the land on Earth, except Antarctica, is divided into countries. There are almost 200 countries in the world!

We live in the United States of America. What are the names of some other countries where people live?

Geography

History

Fast Fact 72

General Sherman tree in California is the world's largest living tree. It stands as tall as a 27-story building.

What do you think you would look like standing next to General Sherman tree? Draw a picture to show your answer.

Fast Fact 73

Hawaii is the only state that grows pineapples and coffee.

What crops grow in your state?

Economics

Fast Fact 74

The White House has six levels—two basements, two public floors, and two floors for the First Family. Visitors are able to see the public floors but not where the First Family lives.

Who is the First Family? Tell what you know about each person.

Fast Fact 75

Long ago, people who lived near the Pacific Ocean carved trees into totem poles. They turned the wood into amazing faces and figures to help them remember stories of their people.

How do people today remember stories that they want to retell?

Culture

Geography

Fast Fact 76

Brazil is the largest country in South America.

What ocean is near Brazil?

Fast Fact 77

Cats were on the *Mayflower*! The ship carried cats on board to keep mice out of the food supply.

Why was it important to protect the food supply on the *Mayflower*?

History

Economics

Fast Fact 78

In the 1700s the barber groomed men's wigs. A thick, curly wig was a sign of wealth and the wearer was known as a "big wig"!

A barber is a service worker. Who are other service workers?

Fast Fact 79

Thomas Jefferson was the first President to shake hands with people rather than bowing.

Shaking hands is an example of respect. When have you seen people shake hands?

Government Citizenship

Culture

Fast Fact 80

Nashville, Tennessee, is known as the home of country music. The popular radio show, the "Grand Ole Opry," comes from Nashville.

What musical instruments are often used when people play country music?

Fast Fact 81

In just a few hours, you could walk all the way across the tiny country of Liechtenstein. The prince of Liechtenstein lives in a castle.

How would you describe a castle?

Geography

History

Fast Fact 82

George Washington rarely smiled because he had false teeth that fit badly.

Look at a quarter and a one-dollar bill. What expression do you see on George Washington's face?

Fast Fact 83

Fish is Japan's most important resource. The Japanese fishing fleet is the largest in the world.

Find Japan on a map. Why do you think fish is an important resource?

Economics

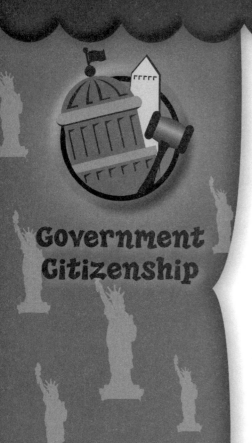

Government
Citizenship

Fast Fact 84

The American flag has many nicknames including "the stars and stripes," "the red, white, and blue," and "Old Glory."

Draw a picture of the American flag.

Fast Fact 85

Many blind people read with their fingers using a system of raised dots called Braille.

How does a seeing-eye dog help a person?

Culture

Geography

Fast Fact 86

Georgia is the largest state east of the Mississippi River.

What state borders Georgia on the west?

Fast Fact 87

Thomas Jefferson, our country's third President, could read books in many different languages and had thousands of books in his personal library.

How do you know that President Jefferson liked to read?

History

Economics

Fast Fact 88

An illustrator is a person who makes the pictures that go in a book. Illustrations can be drawings, paintings, or paper cutouts.

Would you like a job as an illustrator? Tell why or why not.

Fast Fact 89

Laws change over the years. Long ago, in Waterville, Maine, it was against the law to blow your nose in public.

What are some laws that people follow in your community?

Government Citizenship

Culture

Fast Fact 90

Eskimo is the name Europeans gave Inuits. Inuits often lived in tents in the summer, wood and sod huts in the winter, and snowhouses when traveling.

What different materials are used to build homes near you?

Fast Fact 91

In 1850 the trip between London and New York took about three weeks. Now the same distance can be traveled in just over three hours.

What ocean do you cross to go from London, England, to New York City?

Geography

History

Fast Fact 92

Each Pilgrim family on the _Mayflower_ was allowed to bring the family Bible and one chest. The chest held everything the family would need to survive in the new land.

What would you have packed in the chest?

Fast Fact 93

Washington State grows more apples than any other state in the United States.

What color can apples be?

Economics

Government Citizenship

Fast Fact 94

Our nation has people who are in charge. These people make up the government.

What would your school be like if no one was in charge?

Fast Fact 95

During some religious ceremonies in India, elephants are painted and then covered with brightly colored silks and jewels.

What ceremonies have you seen?

Culture

Geography

Fast Fact 96

Where is the river? Indiana's Lost River travels 22 miles underground.

What is the name of one state that borders Indiana?

Fast Fact 97

Benjamin Franklin founded the first public library and the first public zoo in the United States. Both were located in Philadelphia.

How do you know that Benjamin Franklin was a good citizen?

Economics

Fast Fact 98

Paper money is printed on big sheets of paper and then cut into the size that fits into your pocket.

Whose picture is on a one-dollar bill?

Fast Fact 99

The bald eagle is a symbol of the United States. The word *bald* comes from the word *piebald,* which means, "marked with white."

What is one other symbol of the United States?

Government Citizenship

Culture

Fast Fact 100

The Mall of America in Bloomington, Minnesota, is the size of 78 football fields.

What is a shopping mall?

Fast Fact 101

The world is shaped more like a tangerine than a ball. It is a little flat at the North and South Poles.

Look at a globe. What are the large blue areas called?

Geography

History

Fast Fact 102

The world's first skyscraper was built in Chicago in 1885.

Why do you think some buildings are called skyscrapers?

Fast Fact 103

Coin factories are called mints. The United States Mint is the world's largest manufacturer of coins and medals.

What is a medal?

Economics

Fast Fact 104

Independence Hall in Philadelphia is a symbol of our country's beginning because this is the place where the Declaration of Independence was signed in 1776.

What does the word *independence* mean?

Fast Fact 105

States have holidays too. Oklahoma celebrates Bird Day, Utah celebrates Pioneer Day, and people in Nebraska plant trees on Arbor Day.

Imagine a special holiday in your state. What would you name your holiday and how would you celebrate?

Culture

Geography

Fast Fact 106

From the top of the Sears Tower in Chicago, a person can see the states of Illinois, Indiana, Michigan, and Wisconsin.

What lake do you think you could see?

Fast Fact 107

A baby pigeon is sometimes called a squeaker! Long ago, during wartime, pigeons were used for sending messages.

What are some ways that people send messages today?

History

Economics

Fast Fact 108

A port is a place where ships and boats can load and unload. The busiest port in the United States is the Port of South Louisiana.

Freighters carry goods and oil tankers carry oil. What do passenger ships carry?

Fast Fact 109

Citizens of the United States have certain freedoms including the freedom of speech and the freedom of religion. Many of these freedoms are listed in a document called the Bill of Rights.

What do you think it would be like to live in a country that was not free?

Government Citizenship

Culture

Fast Fact 110

Of the eleven most common holidays in the United States, six are celebrated on Mondays to give people a long weekend.

What days are usually included in a long weekend?

Fast Fact 111

Of the original 13 colonies, Pennsylvania was the only colony that did not border the ocean.

Find Pennsylvania on a map. What ocean did the original 13 colonies border?

Geography

History

Fast Fact 112

Many pioneers built their houses with dirt and grass. Unfortunately, the roof often leaked when it rained!

What is a pioneer?

Fast Fact 113

Kansas produces more wheat than any other state.

What are some foods that are made from wheat?

Economics

Government Citizenship

Fast Fact 114

In 1647 Massachusetts required every town of at least 50 families to build a school and hire a teacher.

Why are schools important to a community?

Fast Fact 115

In the United States, more people get married in June than any other month.

What can you tell about wedding celebrations?

Culture

Fast Fact 116

On a map or a globe, the country of Italy looks like a large boot.

On what continent is Italy located?

Fast Fact 117

When Benjamin Franklin wrote, he used a pen called a quill made from a feather. He had to dip the quill in ink each time he used it, which made writing very slow.

What do people use to write today?

History

Economics

Fast Fact 118

Meat from a hog is called pork. Hogs are also used to make brushes, soap, glue, leather, and medicine.

What is meat from a cow called?

Fast Fact 119

Congress, the part of the government that makes laws, meets in a building called the Capitol. "C" is for Congress and "C" is for Capitol too!

Where is the Capitol building located?

Government Citizenship

Culture

Fast Fact 120

When the *Nutcracker* ballet was first performed in Russia more than 100 years ago, it was a big flop! Now it is so popular that it is danced in many places every year at holiday time in December.

What do you call a woman who dances in a ballet?

Fast Fact 121

A large number of volcanoes and earthquakes happen around the shores of the Pacific Ocean. This area is sometimes called the Ring of Fire.

How many states can you name that touch the Pacific Ocean? Name them.

Geography

Fast Fact 122

A baby was born aboard the *Mayflower* as the ship sailed to America. He was named Oceanus.

Is Oceanus a good name for a baby born on the *Mayflower*? Why or why not?

Fast Fact 123

The Chinese invented paper money more than 4,000 years ago. The paper was made from the mulberry tree and printed with blue ink.

What colors do you see on paper money today?

Economics

Government Citizenship

Fast Fact 124

Franklin Delano Roosevelt is the only President of the United States to be elected four times.

How do you know that people thought Franklin Roosevelt was a good President?

Fast Fact 125

Australia is the home of some animals that you will not find on any other continent. These animals include the kangaroo, wallaby, and duckbill platypus.

What do you know about a kangaroo?

Culture

Geography

Fast Fact 126

The Arctic Ocean is the smallest ocean. Ice covering the Arctic Ocean is called sea ice because it forms from frozen seawater.

Look at a globe. Is the Arctic Ocean found at the top or the bottom of the globe?

Fast Fact 127

Ice cream cones were first invented in 1904 at the St. Louis World's Fair.

What is your favorite flavor of ice cream?

History

Economics

Fast Fact 128

Dollars cannot be ripped easily because they are printed on very strong paper made of cotton and linen threads.

What might happen if dollars were printed on the kind of paper you use at school?

Fast Fact 129

Benjamin Franklin wanted the turkey to be the national symbol for the United States instead of the bald eagle.

On what coin is the bald eagle pictured?

Government Citizenship

Culture

Fast Fact 130

In Canada Thanksgiving is celebrated in October.

When do people in the United States celebrate Thanksgiving?

Fast Fact 131

The largest underground cave in the world, about 300 miles long, is the Mammoth-Flint Cave system in Kentucky.

What state is south of Kentucky?

Geography

Fast Fact 132

Before electric lighting, streets were lit by gas lamps. A person called a lamplighter would walk around lighting the gas lamps each day before dark.

What do you think a person called a wheelwright did?

Fast Fact 133

Coins first had ridges around the edges to prevent people from shaving off small bits of gold or silver.

Why would people shave off small bits of gold or silver?

Economics

Government
Citizenship

Fast Fact 134

Only a person born in the United States can become President or Vice President of the United States.

Do you think that this is a good law? Why or why not?

Fast Fact 135

Many Native Americans participate in powwows. These celebrations are focused on dancing.

What other kinds of dancing can you tell about?

Culture

Geography

Fast Fact 136

The Mississippi River begins at Lake Itasca in Minnesota. A person can walk across the river there because it is so narrow and shallow.

What country does Minnesota touch on the north?

Fast Fact 137

Candy was first made in Egypt about 3,000 years ago. Ancient Egyptians used honey instead of sugar to make candy.

What does the word *ancient* mean? Use the word *ancient* in a sentence.

History

Economics

Fast Fact 138

In 1883, when the Brooklyn Bridge opened in New York City, people had to pay three cents to cross it until it was paid for. Now you can cross the Brooklyn Bridge for free.

Do you think it was a good idea to ask the people who used the bridge to help pay for it? Why or why not?

Fast Fact 139

The Library of Congress is one of the largest libraries in the world. It fills more than three buildings.

What could you find in a library other than books?

Government
Citizenship

Culture

Fast Fact 140

The city of Venice in Italy has no streets, only canals. People get around in boats called *gondolas* instead of by car or bus.

How do you move around the community where you live?

Fast Fact 141

Many people in New Zealand call their nation "shaky country" because about 400 earthquakes rock it each year.

North Island is one island that makes up New Zealand. What is the name of the other island?

Geography

History

Fast Fact 142

The first kindergarten in America was opened in Wisconsin in 1856.

How old are most children when they begin kindergarten?

Fast Fact 143

A million dollars in quarters would weigh about as much as a whale.

How many quarters do you need to equal one dollar?

Economics

Fast Fact 144

President Jimmy Carter's daughter, Amy, had a tree house on the lawn of the White House. Sometimes she watched special ceremonies from there.

What do you think it would be like to be the child of a President?

Fast Fact 145

Some snails are very good to eat! The French call a snail that is used for food *escargot*.

Menu is also a French word. What is a menu?

Culture

Geography

Fast Fact 146

Russia has the largest land area of any country in the world. It covers parts of two continents.

Russia covers parts of what two continents?

Fast Fact 147

America is named after an Italian explorer, Amerigo Vespucci, who lived from 1451 to 1512.

What year were you born?

History

Economics

Fast Fact 148

A harvest moon is said to be so bright that farmers can harvest crops by its light.

What does *harvest* mean?

Fast Fact 149

The first daily newspaper was published in Philadelphia on September 21, 1783.

Why are newspapers so important that they have been around for more than 200 years?

Government Citizenship

Culture

Fast Fact 150

The Hawaiian alphabet has only 12 letters.

How many letters does the English alphabet have?

Fast Fact 151

The center of the Arctic Ocean is permanently covered by a layer of ice that grows larger in the winter and shrinks in the summer.

Why do you think the layer of ice shrinks in the summer?

Geography

History

Fast Fact 152

George Washington's home, Mount Vernon, and Thomas Jefferson's home, Monticello, are both located in Virginia.

George Washington and Thomas Jefferson both held the same job. What was it?

Fast Fact 153

In 1910, movies were silent. The average cost of a ticket was seven cents.

Do you think movie actors were paid more or less than they are today? Why?

Economics

Government
Citizenship

Fast Fact 154

The Vietnam Memorial is a long, black granite wall. Engraved on it are the names of the people who did not return from the Vietnam War.

What two holidays honor the people who fought in our country's wars?

Fast Fact 155

Most people in China do not own a car. They usually travel by train, bicycle, bus, river barge, or ferry.

What different kinds of transportation move people from place to place?

Culture

Geography

Fast Fact 156

The name *Utah* comes from the Native American Ute tribe and means "people of the mountains."

What mountains are located in Utah?

Fast Fact 157

Grover Cleveland was the only person to be President of the United States two different times. He was elected in 1884 and again in 1892.

How does a person become President?

History

Economics

Fast Fact 158

Baseball cards were first sold in 1887.

About how long have baseball cards been sold?

Fast Fact 159

Private schools in England are called *public schools*. Public schools are known as *state schools*.

What is the name of your school?

Government
Citizenship

Culture

Fast Fact 160

The Gathering of Nations is a powwow held each year in New Mexico. Thousands of Native Americans come together to perform traditional dances.

What Native American groups have you learned about?

Fast Fact 161

Nebraska has more miles of rivers than any other state.

What are the names of two rivers in Nebraska?

Geography

History

Fast Fact 162

In 1634 Boston Common became the first public park in America.

What can you tell about a park in or near your community?

Fast Fact 163

Paper is made from wood and other plant materials, such as cotton rags.

What other things come from trees?

Economics

Fast Fact 164

Michigan has a floating post office! The *J.W. Westcott II* is a boat that delivers mail to ships while they are moving on the water.

How is your mail delivered?

Fast Fact 165

The new year celebration in Vietnam is called *Tet*. *Tet* lasts for three days and celebrants set off fireworks on the last day.

What holiday do many people in America celebrate with fireworks?

Culture

Geography

Fast Fact 166

The giant panda lives in parts of China and is not a bear at all. Pandas are related to raccoons!

On what continent is China located?

Fast Fact 167

The first English colony in America was located on Roanoke Island. The colony mysteriously vanished with no trace except for a word carved on a tree.

What is a colony?

History

Economics

Fast Fact 168

Almost all of the wild blueberries in the United States grow in the state of Maine.

Are blueberries goods or a service?

Fast Fact 169

In 1950, the little cub that was to become the National Fire Safety symbol was found trapped in a tree when his home was destroyed by fire. The cub was named Smokey the Bear.

What are ways that people can prevent forest fires?

Government Citizenship

Culture

Fast Fact 170

In many countries around the world, people eat in the continental style. This means they keep their fork in the left hand and the knife in their right.

In which hand do you hold your fork?

Fast Fact 171

The island of Greenland looks white because it is mostly covered by ice and snow.

Is Greenland closer to the United States or Canada?

Geography

History

Fast Fact 172

Booker T. Washington was a famous educator. In 1901 he was the first African American to be invited to dinner at the White House.

If you had dinner with the President, what would you like to talk about?

Fast Fact 173

Tennessee is known as the Volunteer State.

What is a volunteer?

Economics

Government
Citizenship

Fast Fact 174

The address of the White House is 1600 Pennsylvania Avenue in Washington, D.C.

What is the address of your school?

Fast Fact 175

On December 26 some countries celebrate a holiday called Boxing Day. Originally, the tradition on Boxing Day was to give small, boxed gifts to service workers.

What holiday do you celebrate where gifts are exchanged?

Culture

Geography

Fast Fact 176

The Dead Sea is really a very large lake. It is so salty that no fish can live in the water.

What is a lake?

Fast Fact 177

A *cowcatcher* was a special iron grille attached to the front of early locomotives. It was designed to prevent accidents caused by cows wandering onto the railroad tracks!

What is the difference between a passenger train and a freight train?

History

Economics

Fast Fact 178

The Model A Ford came on the market in 1927. It was available in four colors and cost $395.00.

What natural resource is needed to make cars run?

Fast Fact 179

The East Room of the White House is often used for special ceremonies. Past Presidents have used this big room for wrestling, boxing, and skating events.

When do the President and his family have to move out of the White House?

Government Citizenship

Culture

Fast Fact 180

People in the Netherlands sometimes wear wooden shoes to protect their feet from the damp earth. These Dutch shoes are called *klompen*.

Why does *klompen* seem like a good name for a wooden shoe?

Fast Facts Answers

1. Alaska and Hawaii
2. Answers may include signing out the book and having it marked with a due date.
3. Answers may include penny, nickel, and some quarters.
4. Answers should include child's name, street address, city or town, and state. Use this opportunity to make children aware of postal Zip Codes.
5. Answers may include seeing family or friends, eating special foods, or staying up late to "ring in the New Year."
6. blue
7. Answers may include not staying in one place long enough or having to work to help support the family. Long ago there was an absence of free public schools.
8. Answers may include a grocery store or farmer's market.
9. Answers may include being ticketed, fined, or arrested.
10. the bald eagle
11. Answers will vary from state to state.
12. Teddy or Ted
13. Answers may include objects that are small, easy to carry around, readily available, or valuable.
14. seven red, six white
15. Answers may include parades, weddings, or other celebrations.
16. the Atlantic Ocean
17. by a small ship
18. a dime
19. Answers will vary.
20. Answers may include wood, brick, or stone.
21. Answers may include Los Angeles, San Francisco, San Diego, San Jose, Sacramento, or others.
22. the *Mayflower*

23. Answers will vary but may include grapes or flowers.
24. Answers will vary but should include an ellipse, or egg shape, drawn around a desk, chair, or other objects commonly found in an office.
25. a building where people go to look at interesting things; a building that displays a collection of objects
26. Rhode Island
27. Answers will vary but may include that cars look different, are safer, can travel at higher speeds, and run better with the help of computers.
28. The motto appears on the top front of a penny and on the bottom left front of a dime.
29. Child should correctly name the current President.
30. green
31. Answers may include the Pacific Ocean, Atlantic Ocean, Gulf of Mexico, or another body of salt water.
32. hard to understand signs, books, newspapers, advertisements, or directions; unable to write signatures, checks, or letters
33. Answers may include that computers are much smaller and can be used to help people communicate, learn, and organize information.
34. Answers will vary but should reflect the importance of keeping people informed.
35. Answers will vary.
36. Washington, D.C.
37. July 4
38. Answers will vary but may include setting the table, clearing the table, and picking up belongings.
39. Answers may include to identify a person who has broken a law or to find a person.
40. Answers will vary but should be related to news.
41. the South Pole
42. Washington, D.C.

43. Answers may include construction workers, business workers, restaurant workers, store clerks, or delivery people.

44. to make a choice about something, to cast a ballot

45. Answers may include rides, shows, games, or food vendors.

46. maple trees; specifically sugar maple trees

47. men no longer wear short pants; the President usually wears a suit and tie

48. George Washington

49. Answers may include that laws help keep us safe.

50. Answers may include cowboys, rodeo clowns, horses, or other animals.

51. Lake Erie

52. Answers will vary.

53. Answers may include penny, nickel, dime, quarter, half dollar, and dollar coin.

54. Answers may include reciting the Pledge of Allegiance, displaying the flag, standing to sing "The Star-Spangled Banner," or taking down the flag during rainy or snowy weather.

55. Answers will vary, but children may suggest that *potato chips* describe the product better than *Saratoga chips.*

56. Mexico

57. Answers may include stuffed toys, musical instruments, models, or paper dolls.

58. Answers will vary.

59. a torch

60. hello, good-bye (*Aloha* is used as both a greeting and a farewell.)

61. the Gulf of Mexico and the Atlantic Ocean

62. Answers may include fire trucks that can reach fires quickly; hydrants, or large water pipes with places where firefighters can connect hoses; building sprinkler systems; or getting help quickly by calling 911.

63. Answers may include peanut butter, peanut oil, peanut brittle, and so on.

64. to celebrate our country's independence, or freedom

65. Answers will vary.

66. Answers may include Houston, Dallas, Fort Worth, Amarillo, San Antonio, and Lubbock.

67. the Potomac River

68. A nickel is now larger than a dime although it is still worth five cents or half a dime.

69. Answers may include to be careful or thoughtful about something; to honor or admire a person; to be polite; or to be understanding of differences.

70. Answers may include hamburgers, hot dogs, French fries, and so on

71. Answers should correctly reflect the names of countries.

72. Drawings should demonstrate an understanding of the great size difference between this tree and a small child.

73. Answers will vary from state to state.

74. Answers may include the names of and facts about members of the President's family.

75. Answers may include writing them down or recording them.

76. the Atlantic Ocean

77. Answers may include that there was no way to get supplies so the food the Pilgrims brought on board had to last through the voyage.

78. Answers may include firefighters, police officers, food servers, paramedics, teachers, nurses, store clerks, and so on.

79. Answers may include when greeting a person or when being introduced to a person.

80. Answers may include guitar, fiddle, or banjo.

81. Answers may include that castles are large buildings, often made of stone, with towers, turrets, moats, and drawbridges.

82. Answers may include somber, not smiling, or serious.

83. Japan is surrounded by water and fish live in water. The Sea of Japan and the Pacific Ocean border Japan.

84. Drawings will vary but should be correctly colored red, white, and blue and show stars and stripes.

85. Answers may include that a seeing-eye dog helps visually impaired people move through crowds; travel; cross streets; and go to work.

86. Alabama

87. Thomas Jefferson owned many books and could read in many different languages.

88. Answers will vary.

89. Answers may include traffic laws, environmental laws, or personal safety laws.

90. Answers may include wood, stone, brick, concrete, or stucco.

91. Atlantic Ocean

92. Answers may include clothes, tools, food, bedding, seeds, or a favorite toy.

93. red, yellow, green

94. Answers may include that it would be confusing because everyone would make their own rules.

95. Answers will vary.

96. Answers may include Illinois, Kentucky, Ohio, or Michigan.

97. He made his community a better place to live and helped the citizens of Philadelphia.

98. George Washington

99. Answers may include the Liberty Bell, Uncle Sam, the American flag, or the Statue of Liberty.

100. a shopping center with stores, shops, restaurants, and so on; may be indoor or outdoor; a large walking area for people

101. oceans, continents

102. They are very tall. They are so tall they seem to touch the sky.

103. a piece of metal like a coin, given as a prize or an award

104. freedom

105. Answers will vary.
106. Lake Michigan
107. Answers may include by mail, telephone, fax, two-way radios, or e-mail.
108. people
109. Answers will vary but may include that people would be told where to work, live, worship, and attend school. The people would not be able to elect their leaders.
110. Saturday, Sunday, and Monday
111. the Atlantic Ocean
112. Answers may include someone who goes first and prepares the way for others or someone who settles in a new part of the country.
113. Answers may include breads, muffins, cereals, cakes, cookies, pies, and so on.
114. Answers will vary but may include that it is convenient if schools are located in the community; education helps children grow up to be responsible citizens; and schools may be centers for social and athletic activities.
115. Answers will vary.
116. Europe
117. Answers may include pencils, pens, typewriters, or computers.
118. beef
119. Washington, D.C.
120. a ballerina
121. Answers may include California, Oregon, Washington, Alaska, and Hawaii.
122. Answers will vary. *Oceanus* means "from the ocean."
123. combinations of green and black
124. He was elected four times.
125. Answers may include that a kangaroo has small front legs and strong hind legs, which give it great leaping power; that it has a strong tail for balance and support; and that the female has a pouch in front for carrying her young.
126. top
127. Answers will vary.